M257 Unit 8
UNDERGRADUATE COMPUTING

Putting Java to work

Threads

Unit
8

This publication forms part of an Open University course M257 *Putting Java to work*. Details of this and other Open University courses can be obtained from the Student Registration and Enquiry Service, The Open University, PO Box 197, Milton Keynes MK7 6BJ, United Kingdom: tel. +44 (0)870 333 4340, email general-enquiries@open.ac.uk

Alternatively, you may visit the Open University website at http://www.open.ac.uk where you can learn more about the wide range of courses and packs offered at all levels by The Open University.

To purchase a selection of Open University course materials visit http://www.ouw.co.uk, or contact Open University Worldwide, Michael Young Building, Walton Hall, Milton Keynes MK7 6AA, United Kingdom for a brochure. tel. +44 (0)1908 858785; fax +44 (0)1908 858787; email ouwenq@open.ac.uk

The Open University
Walton Hall, Milton Keynes
MK7 6AA

First published 2007. Second edition 2008.

Edited, designed and typeset by The Open University.

Printed and bound in the United Kingdom by Hobbs the Printers Ltd.

ISBN 978 0 7492 1993 2

2.1

The paper used in this publication contains pulp sourced from forests independently certified to the Forest Stewardship Council® (FSC®) principles and criteria. Chain of custody certification allows the pulp from these forests to be tracked to the end use (see www.fsc-uk.org).

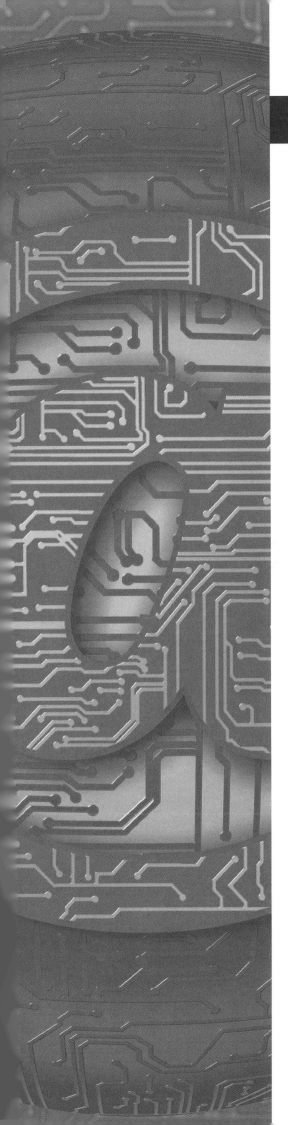

CONTENTS

M257 COURSE TEAM

M257 *Putting Java to work* was adapted from M254 *Java everywhere*.

M254 was produced by the following team.

Martin Smith, Course Team Chair and Author

Anton Dil, Author

Brendan Quinn, Author

Janet Van der Linden, Academic Editor

Barbara Poniatowska, Course Manager

Ralph Greenwell, Course Manager

Alkis Stavrinides, External Assessor, Coventry University

Critical readers

Pauline Curtis, Associate Lecturer

David Knowles, Associate Lecturer

Robin Walker, Associate Lecturer

Richard Walker, Associate Lecturer

The M257 adaptation was produced by:

Darrel Ince, Course Team Chair and Author

Richard Walker, Consultant Author and Critical Reader

Matthew Nelson, Critical Reader

Barbara Poniatowska, Course Manager

Ralph Greenwell, Course Manager

Alkis Stavrinides, External Assessor, Coventry University

Media development staff

Andrew Seddon, Media Project Manager

Garry Hammond, Editor

Ian Blackham, Editor

Anna Edgley-Smith, Editor

Jenny Brown, Freelance Editor

Andrew Whitehead, Designer and Graphic Artist

Glen Derby, Designer

Phillip Howe, Compositor

Lisa Hale, Compositor

Thanks are due to the Desktop Publishing Unit of the Faculty of Mathematics and Computing.

1 Introduction

It is often the case that you would like a program to be able to do more than one thing at a time. You might, for example, want to monitor the keyboard for a key being pressed by a user and, at the same time, track the movement of the mouse by the user and repaint the screen. Each of these tasks can be thought of as a single **thread** in a program. These threads all exist in the same executing environment and so are not the same as different programs. They are separate activities within a program, each of which has a beginning and an end. So far, all of the programs that you have written have had only one thread in them and this has been the thread started by the `main` method. So in *Unit 7* for example, in the ball and paddle game, the control of the paddle and the movement of the ball were competing for the computer's resources and this gave the game a jerky action. What we would really have liked to do is have the paddle control and the ball motion working independently of each other. We can achieve this by making each of these tasks into a thread. Each of these threads can then be running simultaneously, each being between their start and finish at any point in time. Threads are not the actual **static code** itself but rather they are the dynamic process of executing that code.

The concepts surrounding the use of threads are a very important part of large-scale programming and are concerned with an area of computer science known as concurrent systems. Briefly, a **concurrent system** consists of a collection of separate activities or tasks that are simultaneously at some stage between their starting and finishing point. There is, of course, a great deal more to say about concurrent systems but this simple definition will suffice here.

Java provides a great deal of support to the creation of such independent activities or tasks. Each task is made into a thread and on a multiprocessor computer, each thread can truly run at the same time as all of the other threads (up to the number of processors available, of course). However, on a single-processor computer, the CPU can carry out only one set of instructions at a time. In this situation the threads share the CPU, and the operating system will allocate small blocks of time to each thread. This gives the illusion to each thread that it has sole access to the CPU.

As well as making programs more responsive, threads can also be very useful in making use of the times when a processor is idle because it is waiting for something to happen.

Examples of this are as follows:

▶ a program waiting for the user to key in some characters from a keyboard;

▶ a program awaiting the retrieval of data from a disk drive, a mechanical device that can take many milliseconds to carry out its work;

▶ the delay that occurs when the frames of an animation are being loaded.

Threading is an approach to sharing the resources of a computer in such a way that when a particular thread can no longer continue executing or when it has used up its allocated block of time, another thread can begin executing. When this thread is held up, another thread – perhaps even the one that was originally held up – can be executed.

So threads allow programs to give the impression of being able to do many things simultaneously and also enable the program to make best use of the CPU resources that are available.

In this unit, we aim to:

► introduce the idea of concurrent programming – sharing the resources of a computer between a number of threads;

► show how threads can be used to resolve common programming problems;

► give you an overall view of threaded programming;

► show how to avoid problems that can arise when resources are shared between a number of competing threads.

2 Creating threads

A thread is treated as an object in Java and the Thread class is found in the java.lang library. The Thread class has a number of methods for creating, destroying and modifying threads.

Threaded classes can be defined in two ways: by inheriting from the Thread class or by implementing the Runnable Java interface.

Threads are associated with the java.lang package, which is imported automatically.

2.1 Extending the **Thread** class

When using threads, the general approach is first to define a class by extending the Thread class and overriding the run method. In the run method, you should write the code that you wish to run when this particular thread has access to the CPU. Once you have defined your thread class, you can then create an instance of it and set the instance running using the start method that is defined in Thread.

An example of a thread definition, called WhereAmI, using inheritance from the Thread class is shown below:

```
public class WhereAmI extends Thread
{
    int thisThread;

    // constructor
    public WhereAmI (int number)
    {
        thisThread = number;
    }

    // override the run method
    public void run ()
    {
        for (int i = 0; i < 100; i++)
        {
            System.out.println ("I'm in thread " + thisThread);
        }
    }
}
```

So we might create and use an instance of this class as follows:

```
// create an instance of WhereAmI
WhereAmI example = new WhereAmI (2);

/* Invoke the run method of WhereAmI using the
start method of Thread. */
example.start ();
```

In the case above, this code will print out 100 times that it is thread 2 that is currently running.

From your knowledge of programming so far, this will seem to be a fairly straightforward piece of code – when an instance of this class is created and the `start` method is invoked then you would expect it to print to the screen 100 times the string `"I'm in thread 2"` (or whatever value was passed to the constructor). However, as we shall see shortly, this may not be the case.

An example involving three threads is shown below:

```
public class ThreadTester
{
    public static void main (String[] args)
    {
        // create the threads
        WhereAmI place1 = new WhereAmI(1);
        WhereAmI place2 = new WhereAmI(2);
        WhereAmI place3 = new WhereAmI(3);

        // start the threads
        place1.start();
        place2.start();
        place3.start();
    }
}
```

The class `ThreadTester` creates three instances of the `WhereAmI` class. Each instance is passed a different value so that we can identify which thread is running at any particular time. So the first three lines of code in `main` create the three threads. The next three lines of code call the `start` method of each thread to invoke the `run` method of each `Thread` object. The `run` method is never invoked directly by the programmer, but is invoked by the Java run-time system. You might have expected that the code in the `place1` instance would run first, followed by `place2` and then `place3`. A segment of a typical output is given below:

```
I'm in thread 3
I'm in thread 1
I'm in thread 3
I'm in thread 1
I'm in thread 3
I'm in thread 1
I'm in thread 3
I'm in thread 2
I'm in thread 3
I'm in thread 2
I'm in thread 3
I'm in thread 2
```

Activity 8.1
Running the hare and the tortoise race.

We can see here that no one thread had exclusive access to the CPU for its entire execution. One thread has access for a certain amount of time and then another thread has access, and so on. What you will also see is that it is not the case that the threads take it in turns to run. We will look at these more subtle issues later in this unit.

2.2 Implementing the **Runnable** interface

Defining threads by extending the `Thread` class is satisfactory if you wish to inherit from only one class. However, for many applications you will want to inherit from another class as well as from `Thread`. As Java does not allow multiple inheritance, there is an alternative approach to defining a thread, using the `Runnable` interface. This is an interface that contains just one method, `run`. To create the `WhereAmI` thread that we created previously using the `Runnable` interface all we need do is write:

```
public class WhereAmIRun implements Runnable
{
    int thisThread;

    // constructor
    public WhereAmIRun (int number)
    {
        thisThread = number;
    }

    // implement the run method
    public void run ()
    {
        for (int i = 0; i < 100; i++)
        {
            System.out.println("I'm in thread " + thisThread);
        }
    }
}
```

The code above is identical to the code used earlier, except that rather than extending the `Thread` class we are now implementing the `Runnable` interface, which contains just the signature of the `run` method. As there is only the signature of `run` in the `Runnable` interface when we add the code to `run`, we are implementing the method rather than overriding it as we were before.

The `Runnable` interface does not contain a `start` method and so we have an extra step to perform before we can use the class to create a thread. To create a thread from this object, we need to first create an instance of `WhereAmIRun` and then pass it to the `Thread` class constructor. This will create a thread with a `start` method that can be used as before to activate it.

```
public class ThreadTesterRun
{
    public static void main (String[] args)
    {
        // create a runnable object
        WhereAmIRun place1 = new WhereAmIRun(1);

        // now create a thread to run it
        Thread thread1 = new Thread(place1);
```

```
                    // repeat for two further objects
                    WhereAmIRun place2 = new WhereAmIRun(2);
                    Thread thread2 = new Thread(place2);
                    WhereAmIRun place3 = new WhereAmIRun(3);
                    Thread thread3 = new Thread(place3);

                    // start the threads
                    thread1.start();
                    thread2.start();
                    thread3.start();
                }
            }
```

Activity 8.2
Running the hare and the
tortoise race again.

Activity 8.3
Testing concurrent
animation.

When run, this code will produce the same sort of result as with the thread created by extending `Thread`.

2.3 Thread states

So far we have talked about starting and running threads and having access to the CPU in a very general way. What we need to do now is look at the various states that a thread can be in and how a thread might move from one state to another.

A thread is in one of five states at any moment in time. These are:

▶ initial state;

▶ runnable state;

▶ running state;

▶ blocked state;

▶ finished state.

Figure 1 shows the possible transitions between states.

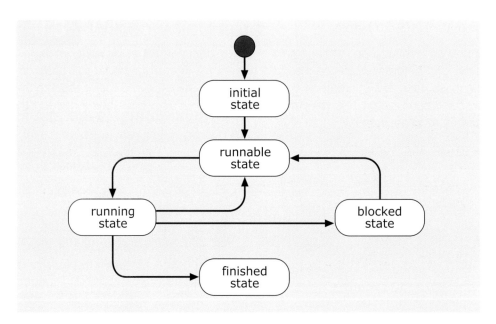

Figure 1   Thread states showing possible transitions

Movement from one state to another is governed by a number of methods which are inherited from the `Thread` class and the `Object` class, as well as by the operating system and other external factors. We have already met some of these methods, but there are others that we will use in order to make full use of threads.

These methods allow some control over which state a thread is in, although you must be aware that the operating system can also change the state of a thread and so your program must anticipate this possibility.

Figure 2 shows a thread which is put into the **initial state** by means of it being created using `new`.

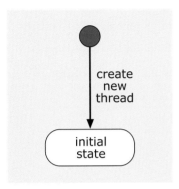

Figure 2   Transition to the initial state

In Figure 3, we see that the `start` method moves the thread into the **runnable state**. This does not mean that it will run immediately (there may be another thread that is being run by the CPU).

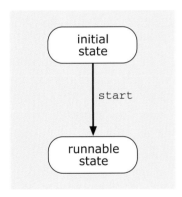

Figure 3   Transition from the initial state to the runnable state

At certain times during the execution of a program that contains threads, the Java system will have a look at all the runnable threads and will select one to execute (which one it selects is discussed later). Only the thread that is actually executing is said to be in the **running state**. This is shown in Figure 4.

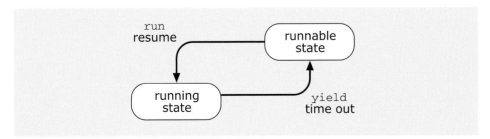

Figure 4   Transitions between the runnable and running states

When a particular thread is chosen, its `run` method is invoked and the thread can begin to execute the code. It is now in the running state. When it finishes executing, it moves into the **finished state** (shown in Figure 5). However, the code may not reach its conclusion before other events intervene. The thread may run out of its allotted CPU time, as represented by the **time out** label in Figure 4. Alternatively, it may invoke the `yield` method to give way to other threads of equal or higher priority. Both scenarios will cause the thread to go back into the runnable state where it can, at some point, be chosen by the Java run-time system to move back into the running state. Once it is back in the running state it can carry on with the execution of its `run` method at the point where it left off. This is indicated by the *resume* label in Figure 4.

We already mentioned that a thread in the running state may run to completion and hence enter the finished state. In Figure 5, we see that it is also possible that a running thread may enter the **blocked state.**

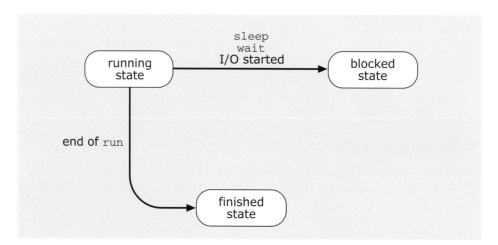

Figure 5   Transitions from the running state to the blocked and finished states

From the running state, a thread may move to the blocked state because of delays in I/O, or because the `sleep` method or `wait` method is invoked. The `sleep` method is a `static` method of `Thread` and so can be called in any program, even those that do not use the `Thread` class. When invoked, it puts the thread to sleep for the specified number of milliseconds. You may recall that we used it in *Unit 7*.

In Figure 6, we see the transition from the blocked state to the runnable state.

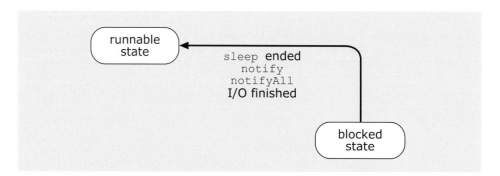

Figure 6   Transition from the blocked state to the runnable state

In the blocked state, the thread cannot progress until something happens – for example, an I/O transfer is completed. Note that from the blocked state the thread can move *only* into the runnable state to await being chosen by the Java run-time system to move into the running state.

Three of the methods that we have seen so far have not been discussed in any detail and they are `wait`, `notify` and `notifyAll`. All three methods are inherited from the `Object` class rather than the `Thread` class, and we will see why this is so later. Briefly, the `wait` method causes a thread to wait for notification by another thread, and `notify` and `notifyAll` provide such notification. The situation is more complicated than this but we will look at it in detail in Section 3.

There are other ways of changing the state of a thread, and later in this unit we will describe them. The important concept at this stage is that a Java program may involve a number of threads, some of which are runnable and ready to be executed by a processor and others that are unable to proceed because they are blocked. On a single-processor machine only one thread can actually be running at a time. The Java system has a component known as the **scheduler** that makes decisions about which thread to run next. The decision as to when thread execution is switched will depend on the underlying operating system: some operating systems switch when the currently running thread becomes blocked, while others allocate set blocks of time to a thread.

Thread priorities

How does the scheduler in the Java system make a decision about which thread to run? The answer is that threads are given a priority between 1 and 10. These are contained in the `Thread` class as static constants `MIN_PRIORITY` and `MAX_PRIORITY` with the former having the value 1 and the latter having the value 10. A thread inherits the priority of its creator; the `main` method (from which, ultimately, all threads come into existence) has by default a priority of 5. This is implemented in the `Thread` class as the constant `NORM_PRIORITY`. The priority of threads can be changed dynamically by invoking the `setPriority` method of the thread.

The decisions made by the scheduler to change a thread from the runnable to the running state can be quite complex. In essence these decisions are platform dependent, which means that the schedulers for the different platforms all have their own set of rules for selecting a thread.

Although of interest, in practice you will find that it is not often you need to set priorities. Indeed, any program logic that relies on priorities set by the programmer will be flawed because priority ranges and implementation are platform dependent.

SAQ 1

(a) What are the two ways to define threads?

(b) When a thread is executing, does it continue executing until it gets to the end of its code?

(c) How do you tell the system that you want to set a thread running?

ANSWERS ....

(a) Threads can be defined by extending the `Thread` class or by implementing the `Runnable` interface.

(b) No, in all likelihood the thread will have access to the CPU for only a short part of its execution before it is stopped and another thread is given an opportunity to run.

(c) After creating an instance of a threaded class, you invoke the `start` method.

SAQ 2

(a) When would you typically want to define a thread by implementing `Runnable` rather than extending `Thread`?

(b) How do you define, create and start a thread using `Runnable`?

ANSWERS ....

(a) There are many occasions when a threaded class will inherit from another class: for example, `JFrame`. As Java does not allow multiple inheritance it is useful to be able to implement an interface to create a thread. Remember, Java allows a class to implement any number of interfaces but to extend only one other class.

(b) The thread class is defined by implementing the interface `Runnable` and the single method in the interface – `run`. You then create an instance of this threaded class and pass this instance to the `Thread` constructor to create a new threaded object. This can then be treated as any other threaded object and can be started by invoking the `start` method.

3 The problem with shared objects

We now have quite a nice toolkit for the manipulation of threads. Unfortunately, our discussion of this toolkit has not mentioned one problem that occurs with threads. It is connected with the topic of shared objects and, in particular, access to shared resources that contain shared data.

The problem of **access to shared resources** is not just a problem that affects Java in particular or even just object-oriented programming languages; it has occurred in programming languages ever since computer hardware first enabled us to share resources amongst a number of processes.

3.1 Accessing shared resources

The problem of accessing shared resources occurs in the overwhelming majority of real-life situations, where there is ultimately one data object being shared by many computers or threads. For example, an airline booking system must, somewhere, have a single record of how many seats on a plane have been booked. Yet that single record must be available to hundreds, if not thousands, of computers in travel agent offices around the world who want to check availability and then book seats for their clients. This is a problem that has always existed for recording systems – even paper-based systems can suffer from this problem.

Consider the following three classes:

```
AirlineBookingTester

NumberOfBookedSeats

TravelAgent
```

The first class, `AirlineBookingTester`, is quite simple and consists of a `main` method. In the `main` method, we create an instance of a class called `NumberOfBookedSeats`. We also create 100 instances of a class called `TravelAgent` which, from the use of the `start` method, we can see is a threaded class. The `main` method then sleeps for a second to allow all of the threads time to complete their processing before printing out the total in `amount`.

```
public class AirlineBookingTester
{
    public static void main (String[] args)
    {
        NumberOfBookedSeats amount = new NumberOfBookedSeats();
        for (int count = 0; count < 100; count++)
        {
            TravelAgent thisone = new TravelAgent(amount);
            thisone.start();
        }
        try
        {
            Thread.sleep(1000);
        }
        catch (InterruptedException e)
```

```
        {
            String errMessage = e.getMessage();
            System.out.println("Error " + errMessage);
        }
        System.out.println("end total = " + amount.getTotal());
    }
}
```

The `NumberOfBookedSeats` class is given below. As well as a constructor that initializes `total` to zero, it consists of three methods – getter and setter methods, which handle access to `total`, and a method called `addOne`, which gets the value of `total`, adds 1 to it, sleeps for a short while to simulate some sort of complex processing or I/O delay, and then uses the set method to update the value of `total`.

```java
public class NumberOfBookedSeats
{
    private int total;
    private int newSum;

    public NumberOfBookedSeats ()
    {
        total = 0;
    }

    public void addOne ()
    {
        newSum = getTotal() + 1;
        try
        {
            Thread.sleep(2);
        }
        catch (InterruptedException e)
        {
            String errMessage = e.getMessage();
            System.out.println("Error " + errMessage);
        }
        setTotal(newSum);
    }

    public int getTotal ()
    {
        return total;
    }

    public void setTotal (int value)
    {
        total = value;
    }
}
```

Finally, we have the `TravelAgent` class, which extends `Thread`. On its creation, it expects to be passed an instance of `NumberOfBookedSeats`. The `run` method is overridden and it invokes the `addOne` method of the `NumberOfBookedSeats` instance.

```java
public class TravelAgent extends Thread
{
    private NumberOfBookedSeats sum;
```

```
    public TravelAgent (NumberOfBookedSeats number)
    {
        sum = number;
    }
    public void run ()
    {
        sum.addOne();
    }
}
```

This sounds fairly straightforward. We create 100 threads, each of which calls a method in an object that adds 1 to a total. Therefore, we would expect the `println` statement in the `main` method at the end to report that end total = 100.

However, when we actually run the code this is not what happens. Instead, the total value typically comes out at between 10 and 23 – it varies with each run. So what is going on here? Not only do we *not* get the answer expected, but the answer that we get varies with each run!

The problem is the use of a shared data object – in this case, it is the single instance of the `NumberOfBookedSeats` class.

So what is wrong with the program? The problem lies in the `addOne` method of `NumberOfBookedSeats`. Each of the threads invokes this method when they are set running. When the `addOne` method is invoked by a particular thread, the following three things happen:

▶ the `getTotal` method is invoked to fetch the current value of `total` and add 1;

▶ the thread then sleeps to simulate some I/O processing;

▶ the `setTotal` method is invoked to update `total` to the new value.

You can imagine that this is like a travel agent first requesting how many seats have been taken on a plane, next adding one person to the number, then having to send the update via a dial-up link and finally the main computer updating its records to show this new addition.

Problems arise because each thread has to share the time with the CPU and so threads are continually being switched between running, runnable and blocked.

Example   Two travel agents

For simplicity let us assume that there are only two threads in the program. The first thread, `travelAgent1`, invokes `addOne`, which in turn invokes `getTotal` to obtain the current value of `total` (which is 0 at the start of the program) and increases it by one. It then becomes blocked (by invoking the `sleep` method in this case). At this point `travelAgent2` is set running by the scheduler. Now `travelAgent2` invokes `addOne`, which in turn leads to `getTotal` being invoked. However, since `travelAgent1` didn't call `setTotal` to record its change in the value of `total`, the second thread `travelAgent2` also finds that the current value is 0 and proceeds to add 1 to `total`. The thread `travelAgent2` now goes into the blocked state and we have both `TravelAgent` threads in the blocked state.

We can assume that the CPU has to deal with many other tasks in the background, such as refreshing the screen so that when the CPU next turns its attention to the `TravelAgent` threads they are both back in the runnable state. However, they are not necessarily moved into the running state in the order that they went into the blocked or runnable state. The selection of which `TravelAgent` thread should move from the runnable to the running state is arbitrary and cannot be decided or determined by the programmer. Whichever `TravelAgent` thread is selected and moved into running, it will carry on from where it left off. If we say that `travelAgent2` was chosen, it will complete by invoking the `setTotal` method and now `total` will have the value of 1. The thread `travelAgent2` then moves into the finished state. In our simplified case, there is now only `travelAgent1` waiting in the runnable state and so it is moved into the running state and it carries on from where it left off. However, it had also found the value of `total` to be 0 and so sets the new value to 1 using `setTotal`. This means that after two `TravelAgent` threads have finished running the new value for `total` is only 1. We have 'lost' one of the updates and this is known as the **lost update problem**. Table 1 summarizes this series of events.

Table 1　The lost update problem

travelAgent1	travelAgent2	total
runnable	runnable	0
running invoke addOne invoke getTotal returns 0	runnable	0
running continue with addOne local variable incremented to 1	runnable	0
running invoke sleep	runnable	0
blocked	runnable	0
blocked	running invoke addOne invoke getTotal returns 0	0
blocked	running continue with addOne local variable incremented to 1	0
blocked	running invoke sleep	0
blocked	blocked	0
runnable	runnable	0
runnable	running invoke setTotal	1
runnable	finished	1
running invoke setTotal		1
finished		1

In our airline example, this means that two people have been booked onto a plane but the system has recorded only one of them. The consequence of this is, of course, that the airline thinks it has more seats that are free than there are really available.

Note that in Table 1 it may appear as if the thread `travelAgent1` has a far longer sleep than `travelAgent2`, and hence stays in the blocked state much longer. This is not the case because the method invocations by `travelAgent2` take up only a fraction of the sleep time.

3.2 Synchronization and locks

The access to shared resources is not just a problem for Java nor even for object-oriented languages in general. It is a potential problem for all systems where shared data is being used. The solution to this particular problem adopted by Java and a number of other programming languages is to designate certain methods that access shared data as **synchronized**. This is achieved by prefacing the method with the Java keyword `synchronized` (note the spelling of this word).

Each object in Java is said to have a **lock**. A thread entering a `synchronized` method gains the lock on the object that contains the method and no other thread can access any `synchronized` method in that object until the lock is released – in this case, by the thread completing the processing inside the method.

We need to ensure that all methods that access the shared data are modified by the keyword `synchronized` because non-synchronized methods can still have access to the shared data if they are invoked. Then, when a thread enters the code of one of the synchronized methods, no other thread can interrupt its processing to gain access to the shared data through synchronized methods: the thread that has entered completes the processing of that method. This is the case even if that particular thread is blocked and, as we shall see in a later section, this in itself can cause significant problems. It is the responsibility of the programmer to ensure that all of the necessary methods are declared as `synchronized`.

During the actual processing, there may be a number of threads trying to access an object. What happens to them? The answer is that the Java system maintains, for each created object that is associated with a class that has `synchronized` methods, a set of threads awaiting permission to access this object – although again, which thread is selected next is arbitrary and not based on any sort of order.

In our particular example program, the problem lies in the `NumberOfBookedSeats` class and, in particular, the methods that access the data field `total`. What we want to be able to do is say that once a thread has entered one of these methods, it will have sole access until it has finished. We achieve this using the keyword `synchronized`.

Below is how we need to modify our program – we simply need to declare the three methods as `synchronized`.

```
public class NumberOfBookedSeats
{
    private int total;
    private int newSum;

    public NumberOfBookedSeats ()
    {
        total = 0;
    }

    // now declared synchronized

    public synchronized void addOne ()
    {
        newSum = getTotal () + 1;
        try
        {
            Thread.sleep (2);
        }
        catch (InterruptedException e)
        {
            String errMessage = e.getMessage ();
            System.out.println ("Error " + errMessage);
        }
        setTotal (newSum);
    }

    public synchronized int getTotal ()
    {
        return total;
    }

    public synchronized void setTotal (int value)
    {
        total = value;
    }
}
```

This small change ensures that once a thread has gained the lock on
`NumberOfBookedSeats`, no other thread can do so until the first thread has released it
by leaving the method. When we run the program now, we get a final value in
`NumberOfBookedSeats` of 100, as we had originally expected.

The general picture on locks is that, in Java, every object contains a lock – this is part of
the class `Object` from which ultimately all objects inherit and it does not require you to
do any coding to create it. Most of the time you don't make use of this facility but when
dealing with threads the lock becomes a valuable tool. As there is only one lock per
object then, even if you have *several* `synchronized` methods in an object, once a
thread has invoked one of them, all other threads are blocked and no thread can access
the other `synchronized` methods until the first one releases the lock. Methods that are
not `synchronized` are not affected by the locking mechanism.

SAQ 3

(a) We saw in the example described in Subsection 3.1 that the expected value for variable `total` of 100 does not materialize. Perhaps more unexpectedly, the answer obtained was not the same each time the program was run. Why might this be?

(b) How were updates lost in the `AirlineBookingTester` program?

ANSWERS ....

(a) The range of answers obtained is a reflection of the arbitrary nature of the choice of thread to be run by the scheduler.

(b) Updates were lost because the scheduler caused one thread to change from the running state to the runnable state before this thread had invoked an important update method. Another thread moved into the running state and completed its update before the first thread had a chance to complete. The first thread then ran from where it left off and updated the values based on the earlier figure it had, and so the second thread's update effectively did not happen.

SAQ 4

How do we ensure that only one thread at a time can execute a method of a particular object?

ANSWER..

By ensuring that all methods of the object that access its variable data fields are `synchronized`. Then once one thread has started executing one of these methods, no other thread can start executing any of the `synchronized` methods on the object until the first thread completes its execution of the method.

Activity 8.4
Running the `GoodThread` and the `BadThread`.

Activity 8.5
Testing locks and objects.

The blocked state

As we have seen, a general description of a thread in the blocked state is that it is a thread that could run but something is preventing it from doing so. While it is in the blocked state it is not allocated any CPU time. It could be blocked because:

▶ it is waiting for an I/O process to complete;

▶ some other part of the program has not completed its processing;

▶ it is not being given access to some shared data.

The last reason is the most interesting from the programmer's point of view, as it is usually something that a programmer can deal with if they are aware that it is occurring.

In Section 3, we saw the problems that can occur when many threads try to work on common data objects. This problem was solved by the use of the `synchronized` modifier. This allowed only one thread at a time to access an object via a `synchronized` method and we saw how the current thread obtained a lock for that object. The lock was released when the thread had completed its processing and then access (or the lock) was available to another thread. In many cases this is an acceptable situation. However, sometimes it is not and there can be very significant consequences. As an illustration we shall look at a situation where problems can arise if we rely simply on synchronization. We will look at the case of a circular buffer. Although it is a little abstract, it is a fairly simple problem that brings out a number of very important points.

4.1 The circular buffer

A **buffer** is a set of memory locations used to store data which is produced and consumed by a number of programs or, in our case, a number of threads. For example, a buffer is used when data is transferred from a user program to a printer: the user program deposits data that is required to be printed into a buffer and the program operating the printer takes the data out of the buffer – usually on a first-in-first-out (FIFO) basis as in the case below. One popular way of implementing a buffer is as a circular queue. This, of course, is only a logical view of the queue; in practice it is implemented in Java using an array. An example of such a queue is shown in Figure 7.

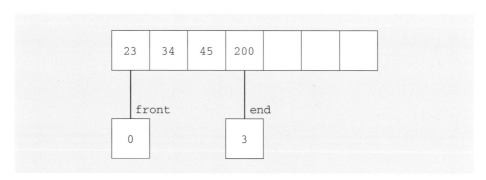

Figure 7   A circular buffer represented by an array

The **circular buffer** is represented as a fixed-length array with two instance variables that point to the beginning and end of the buffer. One variable, front, contains the index to the first item in the buffer and the second variable, end, contains the index to the final item in the buffer.

When an item is removed from the buffer the element indexed by front is updated and the value of the front index is incremented by one. When an item is added to the buffer, the end index is incremented and the item is written to the location at which end now points. If the item to be added overflows the end of the array it is added to the front of the array, provided there is space.

A class describing a circular buffer is shown below. As well as having instance variables for front and end it also has an instance variable numberInBuffer, which contains the current number of items in the buffer, and an instance variable bufferLength, which contains the maximum number of items in the buffer. For the sake of simplicity we shall assume that the buffer contains integers.

```java
public class CircBuffer
{
    private int front, end, numberInBuffer, bufferLength;
    private int [] buffer;

    public CircBuffer (int length)
    {
        buffer = new int [length] ;
        front = 0;
        bufferLength = length;
        end = -1;
        numberInBuffer = 0;
    }

    public CircBuffer ()
    {
        this (100);
    }

    public void addItemToBuffer (int i) throws BufferFullException
    {
        if (numberInBuffer < bufferLength)
        {
            if (end == bufferLength - 1)
            {
                end = 0;
            }
            else
            {
                end++;
            }
            buffer[end] = i;
            numberInBuffer++;
        }
        else
        {
            throw new BufferFullException ();
        }
    }
```

```java
public int removeItemFromBuffer () throws BufferEmptyException
{
    int value;
    if (numberInBuffer > 0)
    {
        value = buffer[front] ;
        if (front == bufferLength - 1)
        {
            front = 0;
        }
        else
        {
            front++;
        }
        numberInBuffer--;
        return value;
    }
    else
    {
        throw new BufferEmptyException ();
    }
}

public int numberInBuffer ()
{
    return numberInBuffer;
}
}
```

The class contains two constructors: one that allows the buffer length to be set to a specific value, the other that defaults the buffer to 100 locations. The class also throws two exceptions – one when the buffer is full and one when the buffer is empty. The code for the exceptions is given below:

```java
public class BufferEmptyException extends Exception
{

    public BufferEmptyException ()
    {
        super();
        System.out.println ("buffer empty");
    }
}

public class BufferFullException extends Exception
{
    public BufferFullException ()
    {
        super();
        System.out.println ("buffer full");
    }
}
```

In order to focus on this problem and its implications, let us concentrate on the method that adds items to the buffer. When the code which sends the current thread to sleep is executed we hope that another thread will remove at least one item from the buffer. When this happens and the current thread awakes from its sleep it can continue executing. Unfortunately, no other thread can do anything to the buffer object since its methods are `synchronized`: only one thread – the one that is sleeping – is allowed access because the sleeping thread still holds the lock. So the solution above does not represent any advance: a thread wanting to add an item to a full buffer cannot do so, even though there may be another thread that is about to remove an item from the buffer.

4.2 Releasing locks

Java provides a solution to this problem in a method which allows a thread to go into the blocked state and to release the hold that it has on a lock. When a thread is sent into the blocked state using the `sleep` method, it *retains* the lock. To get over this problem the `wait` method puts the thread into the blocked state and *releases* the lock that it holds. Threads put into the blocked state can be made runnable using the methods `notify` and `notifyAll`. All of these methods are part of the `Object` class, not the `Thread` class, because every object has a lock even though it is used only by a programmer when dealing with threads.

When a thread accesses an object – for example, to read data – it may have to invoke the `wait` method if it finds that there is no data to be read. Having invoked the `wait` method, the thread then becomes blocked, is placed in a set of threads that are waiting to access the object and *releases* the lock that it held. This gives another thread the chance to *add* an item to the buffer. When the reading thread is activated again, there is now data for it to read.

The `wait` method is associated with two methods known as `notify` and `notifyAll`. One of these methods should be called when the state of an object has changed and the threads in the set for that object can be given a chance to access it.

Invoking a `notify` method informs the scheduler that another thread can now be moved to the runnable state; if it is then selected to become running, it can try to access the object. An important point to note is that the thread selected when the `notify` method is invoked is an arbitrary choice by the scheduler, and will not necessarily be the first thread that began waiting. Invoking the `notifyAll` method will move *all* the threads currently in the blocked state into the runnable state.

The code for the two methods now becomes:

```
public synchronized void addItemToBuffer (int i)
{
    while (numberInBuffer == bufferLength)
    {
        try
        {
            wait();
        }
        catch (InterruptedException e)
        {
            String errMessage = e.getMessage();
            System.out.println("Error " + errMessage);
        }
    }
}
```

```
                    if (end == bufferLength - 1)
                    {
                        end = 0;
                    }
                    else
                    {
                        end++;
                    }
                    buffer[ end] = i;
                    numberInBuffer++;
                    notifyAll ();
            }

            public synchronized int removeItemFromBuffer ()
            {
                int value;
                while (numberInBuffer == 0)
                {
                    try
                    {
                        wait ();
                    }
                    catch (InterruptedException e)
                    {
                        String errMessage = e.getMessage ();
                        System.out.println ("Error " + errMessage);
                    }
                }
                value = buffer[front] ;
                if (front == bufferLength - 1)
                {
                    front = 0;
                }
                else
                {
                    front++;
                }
                numberInBuffer--;
                notifyAll ();
                return value;
            }
```

In both methods, the method `notifyAll` is called after all the work is done, in order to give another thread the opportunity to execute.

This approach translates into a simple set of rules as follows.

▶   If two or more threads modify a common object, then declare the methods that do the modifying as being `synchronized`.

▶   If a thread needs to wait for an object to change, make sure that it waits inside the thread. It does this by entering a `synchronized` method and calling `wait`. In fact, `wait` can be used only inside a `synchronized` method.

▶   When a method has changed an object, it should call the `notify` method or the `notifyAll` method before terminating. This gives other methods a chance to access the object. Like `wait`, the `notify` and `notifyAll` methods can be used only inside a `synchronized` method.

Activity 8.6
Running the greedy consumers.

Activity 8.7
Testing the storage tank.

4.3 Moving all threads to the **runnable** state

As a final topic, we look at the difference between notify and notifyAll. The notify method causes the scheduler to arbitrarily select one of the threads currently waiting in the blocked state for the lock on a particular object and moves it into the runnable state. The notifyAll method causes *all* of the threads currently in the blocked state and waiting for the lock on a particular object to be moved into the runnable state. Remember that being in the runnable state does not mean that a thread will run, but simply that it has the opportunity to be selected to go into the running state. So, superficially, it would seem that there is no difference between notify and notifyAll – the end result is that one of the originally blocked threads will be able to go, at some point, into the running state.

The most important grounds for using notifyAll rather than notify is that it is safer, particularly if we are not entirely sure how threads are interacting with each other.

If notify is called and the single arbitrary thread that gets unblocked is the wrong one, it will find it cannot proceed and call wait again. If it is the wrong thread but proceeds anyway, the system is in an incorrect state. At this point it is possible that none of the runnable threads can make progress, because the conditions are wrong, and the only threads that would have been able to continue are still blocked. The runnable threads then become blocked one by one, until all are blocked never to be released.

Example   Train simulation

The problem of selecting the wrong thread when using notify can be illustrated in a train simulation program. We have an application that uses threads to simulate three trains that must go through a tunnel in strict rotation: 1, 2, 3, 1, 2, 3, ... In this application, a variable turn is used to indicate which train should be allowed next into the tunnel. When a train comes to the tunnel, it tests the value of turn and either proceeds or calls wait as appropriate. A train that traverses the tunnel increments turn cyclically (so that it takes the values 1, 2 and 3 in rotation) and calls notify to signal that it has completed its use of the tunnel.

Now suppose turn is currently at 1 and the trains arrive, as they may do, in the order 2, 3, 1. Train 2 and then train 3 both call wait and are in the blocked state. Train 1 passes through the tunnel, turn is set to 2, and notify is called.

This unblocks one thread at random. The thread released might be train 2, which is the one that *should* go next, but is equally likely to be train 3!

Imagine the scenario where train 3 is picked. When it runs it tests turn, finds that it is set to 2, and blocks again. The only runnable thread is now train 1; when it runs, it *too* is blocked, because it finds that turn is 2. Now all three trains are blocked and remain so because none of the threads can get to a point where they can notify another thread to become runnable. Since the scheduler can select only threads that are runnable, *not* blocked, the application has come to a complete halt.

Using notifyAll solves the problem because not just one but *all* blocked threads are released, and this is bound to include the right one, the thread for train 2. Sooner or later train 2 will then get to run and will successfully travel through the tunnel, increment turn to 3, and call notifyAll. This again releases any threads that are blocked, so we can be sure train 3 will run and find its way through the tunnel. Then turn will become 1 once more and all the waiting threads will be released, effectively starting the whole process over again from the beginning.

The train example has shown that we should use notify if it is important to wake up no more than one thread but it doesn't matter which one. Where we have a more complex situation we should use notifyAll, because this is a safer option.

SAQ 5

(a) What is the difference between a thread in the blocked state and one in the runnable state?

(b) What is the difference between the method sleep and the method wait?

ANSWERS ....

(a) A runnable thread is fully ready to run once it is chosen by the scheduler. On the other hand, a thread in the blocked state is definitely not ready to run because it is waiting for something to happen. It may be waiting either for an I/O event to happen or because the wait method has been invoked.

(b) When a thread invokes the sleep method it holds onto any lock that it has got through having entered a synchronized method. This prevents any other thread getting access to this method (or any other synchronized methods in the same object) while it sleeps. However, with wait, the thread releases the lock it has on the object and so allows other threads to have access while it is waiting.

SAQ 6

In the travel agent flight-booking scenario discussed in Section 3, can you think of a situation where it would be useful to have a wait or notify approach?

ANSWER...

If a flight was full then a travel agent could wait for a cancellation to be notified (all agents might be notified or only one chosen by the airline might be notified).

Activity 8.8
Testing the three game players.

5 Summary

In this unit we have looked at the idea of threads and seen how they allow us to make the best use of the computing resources of a processor. We have described some of the methods of the `Thread` and `Object` classes and how one of the problems that can arise with threads – that of shared access to objects – can be overcome by means of the `synchronized` facility.

We have seen that threads can be in one of five states and that through various methods we have some control over which state a thread is in. However, part of the operating system, the scheduler, also has an important role to play in changing the state of a thread. A key idea that we have met is that of a lock; it is through control of the lock on an object that it is determined which thread has access to a particular object. In *Unit 9*, which deals with communication system programming in Java, you will see threads being put to work extensively.

LEARNING OUTCOMES

When you have completed this unit, you should be able to:

▶ understand how threads can help to make more effective use of a computer's resources;

▶ define, create and use threads;

▶ describe the various states that threads can be in;

▶ appreciate some of the problems that can occur when threads access shared resources;

▶ understand how locks affect the execution of code.

Concepts

The following concepts have been introduced in this unit:

access to shared resources, blocked state, buffer, circular buffer, concurrent system, finished state, initial state, lock, lost update problem, runnable state, running state, `static` code, scheduler, `synchronized`, `Thread`, thread state, time out.

Index